Title: The Ivy League Roadmap
Author: Andreas Stamatakis
Editor: Nicholas Stamatakis
Editor: Vito Nole
Editor: Virginia Stamatakis
Illustrator/Photographer: Sophia Pav

ISBN-13: 9798388143808

Cover design by: Sophia Pav
Library of Congress Control Number: None
Printed in the United States of America

DEDICATION

To my brother, Nicholas, who was the first to test out every strategy in this book.

His phenomenal success is what inspired me to help students from around the world.

CONTENTS

INTRODUCTION

Why should I trust your Advice?

PREAMBLE

Do you even want this?

CHAPTER
1

How to Approach Ivy League Admissions

CHAPTER
2

Who gets into Ivies?

CHAPTER
3

How Ivy League Schools Make Decisions

CONTENTS

CHAPTER

4

Framing Your Application

CHAPTER

5

How to Write a Stellar College Essay

CHAPTER

6

How to Stand Out in Ivy League Admissions

CHAPTER

7

Timeline for Admissions

CONTENTS

CHAPTER

8

What to do before 9th Grade

CHAPTER

9

What to do in 9th Grade

CHAPTER

10

What to do in 10th Grade

CHAPTER

11

What to do in 11th Grade

CHAPTER

12

What to do in 12th Grade

CONTENTS

CHAPTER
13
How to work with Andreas

CHAPTER
14
Transfer Admissions

CHAPTER
15
International Admissions

CHAPTER
16
Frequently Asked Questions

INTRODUCTION

WHY SHOULD I TRUST YOUR ADVICE?

Most "Ivy Admissions Advice" Authors brag about their own Ivy League acceptances and use that to justify the value of their advice.

I won't do that.

Yeah, sure, I got into Ivy League schools, but how does that help you? If you just copied what I did to get in, it wouldn't work. An effective admissions plan is customized to just one person: **YOU.**

My advice isn't worth listening to because it got me into an Ivy League school. It's worth listening to because it has helped 100s of my clients and 1000s of my followers get into every school in the Ivy League, and elite colleges around the world.

They didn't get in by copying me. They got in using the principles I taught them to create a custom strategy and executed on it.

I hope you'll use the Ivy League Roadmap to do the same.

Best,

Andreas Stamatakis

PREAMBLE

DO YOU EVEN WANT THIS?

PREAMBLE - Do You Even Want This?

Long hours. Hard work. Time. Money. Sacrifice. That's what it takes to get into an Ivy League School. The vast majority of Ivy League applicants are doing it for the wrong reasons. They volunteer 100s of hours, waste 1000s of dollars and give themselves an anxiety disorder over something they would regret if they got it. So, before you devote years of your life to this goal, let me tell you a few things an Ivy League School will NOT get you:

- **A Better Education:** Every course you could ever want to take at an Ivy League School is already on YouTube for free. If all you want is to learn, you don't need an Ivy.
- **The Respect of your Peers:** ZERO people will like you better for having attended an Ivy. In fact, you'll have to play it down your whole life or people will call you arrogant and stop being your friend.
- **A Parent's Love:** If you're doing this only to make your Parent(s) happy, please don't. Even if you succeed, you'll build a habit of dependence on their validation and handicap yourself for success in life.

If you're applying to an Ivy for one of those reasons, this book is not for you. Save your time, money and heartache and go to the most affordable college you can get into.

Here's what attending an Ivy **WILL** get you:

- **Instant Credibility for Life:** Anything you say, any business you start, any effort you lead will automatically be taken seriously because you're an "Ivy League Graduate". This is a huge advantage to any career.
- **$100K+ in Savings on College:** If you get into an Ivy League School, you can almost always leverage that acceptance for a full tuition scholarship at a State School. If you do choose to attend the Ivy, their Financial Aid is usually very generous.
- **Access:** Want to interview at Google? Go to a top medical school? Get hired at the highest levels of government? Done, done and done. All of the highest rungs on the ladder will be available to you.

Is that what you're after? Good. Then let's get started.

HOW TO APPROACH IVY LEAGUE ADMISSIONS

CHAPTER 1 - How to Approach Ivy League Admissions

What You'll Learn:
- How Risk Management can get you into an Ivy
- What a 4% acceptance rate REALLY means
- How to pick the right Admissions Advisor.

People can't wrap their minds around what a 4% Acceptance rate really means. To put this in perspective, **in a High School of 600 people, every student could apply to Harvard and if ZERO of them got in, it would be a perfectly reasonable outcome.** Ivy League Admissions is too complicated to predict on the level of an individual school, the same way an investor isn't able to predict the price of an individual stock. Fortunately, savvy investors solved this problem a long time ago with a single tool: Risk Management.

If you want to make a lot of money in the Stock Market, you don't pick a single stock and pray it goes to the moon. Investing is a game of survival. If you just keep from going to "zero" for long enough and have a diversified portfolio, eventually you'll win. **Avoid losing and you win by default.** That's risk management. You can do the same thing with Ivy League Admissions.

Often, families will ask me "can you get my child into Harvard?", my answer? "Absolutely not." **The best Admissions Advisor on the planet (me) can't guarantee an outcome with a particular school any more than Warren Buffet can predict the price of an individual stock.** There are too many factors outside of my control to be able to say that confidently. What I CAN do is provide a Risk Managed plan for Admissions. A strategy that will maximize the chance of success at any school, Ivy or otherwise.

There are two levers you can pull to make this work: 1) Boosting the quality of the applications so the odds at any given school are better and 2) increasing the number of schools you apply to. Risk management is how you decide what helps your application. Should you take the SAT/ACT and score in the top 1%? Well, maybe you can get in without it, but **why risk it?**

CHAPTER 1 - How to Approach Ivy League Admissions

Take the exam and score high. Could you get in without impressive people recommending you? Maybe, but **why risk it?** Get the recommendation. Could you get in without a Professional Writer helping you on your essays? Maybe, if you're unusually talented, but **why find out?** Hire the writer and rest easy.

Key Reframe: Lowering your risk of rejection IS raising your odds of acceptance.

Students who follow my advice and work closely with my team, on average, have a ~30% chance of admission to a given Ivy League school. That's ~5x the average odds of admission. Even so, for any given Ivy they apply to there's at least a 70% chance they get rejected. What does this mean? **You can do everything right, win all the awards, hire the best experts and STILL get rejected from an Ivy.** The "Perfect Application" isn't enough. That's why we diversify.

Diversification is a simple rule. If you want to get into one Ivy, you should apply to ALL the Ivies. Most advisors will tell you to only apply to a school if you "want to go there". But the truth is, ALL schools at the level of an Ivy are so good that you'd be foolish not to go IF the finances work out. If you turn down an Ivy for "bad weather" you have poor judgment. Also, the math backs this approach. The average acceptance rate at an Ivy League School is ~6%. If you apply to all 8 your expectation value is 6% x 8 = 0.48. **The average applicant can apply to all 8 Ivies and STILL have it be more likely than not that they get rejected from ALL of them.** Now imagine you read my book and follow my advice. At minimum you'll ~2x your odds from the average, so doing the same math, 12% x 8 = 0.96. **In plain English, if you do what I say in this book and apply to ALL the Ivies, you have a good chance of getting at least 1, according to the math.** Students who work with me personally have a historical rate of admission around 30%, so doing the same calculation 30% x 8 = 2.4, and on average, they have a good chance of getting into 2 Ivies, with some doing much better.

CHAPTER 1 - How to Approach Ivy League Admissions

A word of caution: **DO NOT** let College Admission determine how you live your life. The strategies and suggestions in this book are left broad on purpose. They're meant to adapt to YOU, so you can focus on the things you're good at, reduce stress, and win all at the same time. With enough creativity, there's a way to frame almost every smart, hard-working kid in a way that they can have a good shot at an elite university. **If you're my client, I want you to focus on building the foundational skills that will make you a successful HUMAN, and if that also gets you into Harvard, that's the cherry on top.**

How to Hire an Ivy League Admissions Advisor

Knowing how to hire the right Admissions Advisor will make or break your application. A good Advisor will 1) tell you EXACTLY what you need to do 2) help you avoid common traps that lead to rejection and 3) reduce the stress of the admissions process. Be sure to look for the following when hiring an Advisor:

1.Student Success, not Personal Success: The best NBA coaches didn't play in the NBA. Similarly, having been admitted to an Ivy League School is NOT by itself a qualification to give advice on Ivy League Admissions. Most Ivy Admissions "Advisors" are Ivy League Grads trying to coast off the brand of the school they attended, and give advice that worked for them but is unlikely to work for YOU. Judge them based on the success of the students they've worked with, not their personal success. That's how you know if their advice is worth anything.

2.Their Advice makes sense, no matter the Source: The best way to weed out BAD college admissions advice is to ask yourself: "Would I be agreeing with this if a stranger told it to me?" Often, Ivy League Admissions Officers (AO) will give advice that's ludicrous on its face like "just be yourself" or "high family income isn't an advantage in admissions" and people will believe it because "the Harvard guy said it". If what they're saying makes NO SENSE if you heard it from a different source, you shouldn't trust them. Former AO's are particularly guilty of this so watch out for that.

3. Clear Plan of Action: Many Admissions "advisors" will take your money, meet with you a few times, then give only vague advice as to what you should do to get in. This doesn't work. If an Advisor can't articulate a specific plan with clear milestones, you need to find another one.

Red Flag: If an Ivy League Admissions Advisor tells you they can **DEFINITELY** get you into a particular school, they're lying or doing something illegal. The best you can do is raise the odds as high as you can and know that hard work always pays off in the end.

Key Takeaways:

- Admissions results at a given school are UNPREDICTABLE.
- Even the best applicants have a ~70% rejection rate.
- Lowering your odds of rejection IS increasing your odds of admission.
- If you want to get into 1 Ivy, you should apply to ALL of them.
- Focus on becoming a successful HUMAN and elite college admissions will follow.
- Make sure your Admissions Advisors meet the highest standards.

CHAPTER 2

WHO GETS INTO IVIES?

CHAPTER 2 - Who gets into Ivies?

What You'll Learn:
- How an Ivy League college makes money
- What an "Ideal" Candidate looks like
- What your Application must show them (if you want **to get in**)

First, a Hard Truth: Ivy League Colleges are a business.

Businesses need money to survive. So, how do Ivy League Colleges make money?

A few main sources:
- Endowments
- Tuition
- Alumni Donations

Every Ivy League school has a multi-billion dollar endowment. This is a fund, like a retirement account, that gets invested in the stock market and pays out annual returns. For schools like Harvard, this endowment is worth $30B+ but only about 3-4% is disbursed to the university in a given year. You'd think this would give Ivies money to blow, but **their expenses are so huge that even with a $1B+ Annual Endowment payout, they are ALWAYS strapped for cash.**

Tuition, particularly for international students who are charged the full rate, makes up a significant part of the operating revenue for an Ivy League school. This is why **you can improve your chances drastically when you check the box on your application that indicates that you will NOT be applying for financial aid.**

Alumni Donations are the fuel that keeps the University engine going. Spend too much on a renovation project? No problem, slap a fresh name on it, collect a $2 Million check and "poof" problem solved. Want to hire another layer of administrators to supervise the ones already there? Fund it in one phone call. Alumni donations are the key to understanding admissions, because **the thing Ivy League Admissions look for is the <u>next generation of successful, generous Alumni Donors.</u>**

CHAPTER 2 - Who gets into Ivies?

A successful application is showing the school 3 things: 1) You're a good person 2) You will be successful (rich or influential in government) and 3) You love the university enough to donate.

What are the qualities of a successful Ivy Applicant?
- **Smart:** 1500+ SAT, 3.8+ GPA in the most rigorous classes available in your school.
- **Talented:** Multiple awards, achievements or recognition at a state or national level for excellence in an area you're capable in.
- **Proactive:** Uses internships, summer programs and clubs to explore the areas he or she would like to study in college so when interest is claimed, it's legitimate.
- **Connected:** Letters of Recommendation come from influential people in Science, Business or Politics.
- **Likable:** The most important quality of your application is that you appear likable to the Admissions Officer. In an application, this does not mean writing about how much fun you had in your summer vacation or how great your teachers are. It means using a narrative that shows the Admissions Officer why they should like you, over any other applicant. Be funny, passionate, caring and above all unique and you'll make them fall in love with you.

This book will show you how to **build on your natural skills and talents** until you have so many impressive attributes that you could fill a dozen applications. Then, we'll show you how to **refine them down to a simple, clear story** that will convince an admissions officer that you deserve a spot in the Ivy League.

Admissions Post-COVID: COVID allowed elite universities to test what admissions would look like in the absence of objective criteria like the SAT/ACT and a lot of them liked it because it gave them the flexibility to admit whichever candidates they "felt" were deserving. The emphasis post-COVID is on "feelings", not objective competence so when given a choice always play to the feelings of an Admissions Officer. They will go out of their way for the applicants they love, and will reject a 1600 SAT student in a heartbeat if he comes off cold, robotic or entitled.

CHAPTER 2 - Who gets into Ivies?

Key Takeaways:

- Ivies are looking for the next generation of Alumni Donors.
- Being Likable is more important than being Smart (but you better be both).
- Having a clear, simple story will help you get in.

CHAPTER 3

HOW IVY LEAGUE SCHOOLS MAKE DECISIONS

CHAPTER 3 - How Ivy League Schools Make Decisions

What You'll Learn:
- How Ivy admissions works on the inside
- Why your AO must LOVE YOU
- Why applying Early can TANK your odds of Admission

How do Ivies decide? Quickly, then slowly by committee.

Admissions offices are **secretive about their exact process** and it varies widely by school even within the Ivy League. However, based on public descriptions by admissions officers, here's the general way an application gets reviewed:

First, **your application gets sent to 2 Admissions Officer (AO) readers who specialize in your region of the country** to be lightly reviewed and scored. This is meant to weed out anyone who applied to an Ivy because "you never know", but is obviously unqualified to go there (about half the applications). The remaining serious applications get scrutinized in a lot of detail. **If you want to know how a specific Ivy will weigh different parts of your application, go on Google and search "<Name of School> CDS".** This will lead you to the Common Data Set for each school which about half way through will include a table telling you how a particular school thinks about different parts of your application.

Once your application is scored (yes it's actually a number) **they prioritize the candidates into tiers based on the likelihood of your admission.** Top tier candidates get their essays, letters etc. read first so they can be sent "likely letters" and other prioritized communications meant to protect yield on admitted students of the incoming class. Once they work through a tier and admit the ones they want, they then start reading the next tier and so on.

CHAPTER 3 - How Ivy League Schools Make Decisions

When it's not obvious if a candidate should be admitted or not (most of the time) the decision will go to a committee which will vote by majority to decide if a candidate gets in. The two admissions officers for your region are the ones responsible for knowing your application in detail and present the case to the whole committee. **Your candidacy is almost entirely based on 1) the strength of the advocacy of your Reader and 2) the number of open spots remaining.**

Most of the work you do on your application will focus on maximizing these last two factors. You take hard classes and get high test scores to pass the first read and land in the top tier (spots still open). You write an amazing essay to make your Reader fall in love with you so they'll go out of their way to advocate on your behalf. You get impressive letters of recommendation for social proof, making the Reader secure in their choice to present you to the committee. **Most of all, you must ensure your application has a clear, simple and strong message that your Reader will understand and present well.**

Note on Children of Celebrities/Donors: If you think the children of Celebrities go through the same admission process as everyone else when applying to Ivies you're kidding yourself. Ivies collect the children of Billionaires, Celebrities and Influential Politicians like trophies because they know how much influence they have. They're picked out of the admissions pool with special attention and given "white gloves" treatment on the spot.

3 Tracks to Admission:

You can apply to an Ivy through Early Action, Early Decision or Regular Decision.
- **Early Action (EA):** Deadline in November and decision by December. Non-binding if accepted, but if you do "Restricted Early Action" for a school you can only submit to that school.
- **Early Decision (ED):** Deadline in November and Decision by December. Binding if admitted, so if you applied to other schools also you'll have to withdraw the apps if accepted.

- **Regular Decision (RD):** Deadline in early January and decision by Late March. Non-binding, much larger (and weaker) applicant pool.

Early Admissions (EA or ED) will differ from Regular Decision in a few key ways:

1. AO's are MUCH more Risk Averse: There is a lot of turnover in Elite Admissions offices, and Early Application cycles are often used to train the new AO's. Since they're new and don't want to be put on the spot for recommending candidates that might not be up to snuff, they're generally much harder graders on the applications they review. Even experienced AO's will hesitate in Early Admissions since they haven't seen the full scope of applications for that year and would prefer to leave spots open for strong candidates in RD. This is why schools like Harvard will defer up to 70% of their EA applicants in a given year.

2. The Competition is STRONGER: Strong applicants are generally proactive and apply early. This includes recruited athletes, national award winners, children of celebrities and true hardship cases that know they have a leg up in admissions. Since your application is always judged in the context of the applications surrounding it, if you apply early, even a 9/10 application can look like a 7/10 when surrounded by 10/10's.

3. Odds of Admission after Deferral are Lower than RD: First impressions last. Most College Counselors will tell students to apply early because the admission rate is higher. This is only true for a minority of students who would be "obvious" admits in any context. For candidates where the process could have gone either way (80%+ of admits) applying early can be detrimental because it forces AO's to judge them in the context of 10/10 applications and almost definitely defer. Once you've been deferred it is VERY HARD to change their mind to admit. They already had a chance to take you and chose not to. You never want to find yourself fighting that kind of inertia. To put this in context, the RD admit rate for Harvard was around 4% in 2022 but the admit rate after deferral is ~1%. Yikes.

Pro Tip: If you know you're a "Borderline" candidate, your odds are MUCH better in RD than EA or ED. Don't get spooked by weak competition and fall into the Lion's Den.

Anticipating some objections to the above, let's clear up some misconceptions about Early Admissions:

1. Elite Schools DO NOT use ED/EA to protect Yield:

You're not doing Harvard a favor by applying early, no matter who you are. They know if you get into Harvard and another school, there is a 90%+ chance you're still going to pick Harvard. This is why Harvard doesn't even have ED, they don't need it. **Ivies don't do Early Admissions for yield**, it just gives them a chance to have a sneak peek at top candidates. Lower ranked schools (think T20 or above) DO use ED/EA to protect yield as without it there is a good chance they would lose top candidates to higher ranked schools in RD.

2. The Admit Rate IS NOT your Odds of Admission: Even smart people get confused by statistics. Just because the overall Yale admit rate is 5.3% doesn't mean YOUR odds of getting into Yale are 5.3%. All it means is "assuming all applications are equal" there's a 5.3% chance of getting in. But NONE of the applications are equal. A strong applicant can have over a 30% success rate at a school like Yale, 5x above the average. **People applying "just for fun" don't have a 5.3% chance, it's just zero.** The same is true for ED/EA where the Admit rates can be 2-3x the general rate for RD, but that doesn't mean it helps borderline candidates the way it helps strong ones. Most Admissions Advisors get this wrong despite good intentions because 1) they generally have a weak math background and get confused by statistics or 2) their practice is focused on lower tier (beyond T20) schools where ED/EA IS an advantage and they don't adjust their advice for students with higher aspirations.

CHAPTER 3 - How Ivy League Schools Make Decisions

Bottom Line: Early Admissions can be a great option for strong applicants, but they should think twice before doing it if they are borderline. The risk of being deferred is too high and once you're in the waiting pool, your odds of admission go down drastically. Before submitting your application early, talk to an admissions advisor who has experience with Ivy League admissions to make sure it's the right option for you.

Deferred/Waitlist: Getting deferred in EA/ED or waitlisted in RD is the purgatory of College Admissions. The only thing you can do to improve your odds at that point is to send a Letter of Continued Interest which describes any new accomplishments and reaffirms your desire to attend that school. To save yourself emotional turmoil, you should treat these as rejections, and if you're lucky enough to be brought off the list, let it be a happy surprise.

Legacies: If you have a direct relative (sibling, parent or grandparent) who attended the college you're applying to, you are a Legacy. This gives you an advantage in Admissions, but only if the odds are close. If you're already a competitive candidate, and they're deciding between you and a non-Legacy, it could be the small push you need to get in. However, since the vast majority of Ivy decisions are close, this can be a very powerful edge.

Key Takeaways:
- Only strong applicants should apply early.
- Your AO is your advocate in Committee, so give them all the ammunition you can.
- 80%+ of Admits are "Borderline" so small details matter.
- The number of open spots will impact your admission as much as the strength of your application.

CHAPTER 4

FRAMING YOUR APPLICATION

CHAPTER 4 - Framing Your Application

What You'll Learn:
- Why being Human is better than being Smart
- Why being modest will HURT your odds
- How a SIMPLE story will get you into an Ivy

When your Regional AO goes to committee they have to give a little speech about you. That speech will 1) summarize your strengths 2) identify your weaknesses and 3) present a case for why you should be admitted (or not).

Wouldn't you rather write that speech yourself?

Framing your application is how you do that. Your application must present a simple, clear narrative that can be summed up in a sentence or two which accomplishes the following:

1. It must Humanize you: AO's favorite kind of rejection is the "one dimensional smart kid". If the only theme of your application is that you get good grades in school and on tests, they will reject you in a heartbeat. Instead, use your extracurriculars and Passion Project (more on this later) to show how you can give back to your community using your talents and empathy. Your essay can share a vulnerable experience that you learned and grew from (use the essay guide in Chapter 13. Use every opportunity in the supplements to focus on the parts of you that are emotional and unique. It's harder to reject a "Human".

2. It must elevate your Accomplishments: One of the most common flaws of high achieving students is that **they think their exceptional accomplishments are "normal"** and will either understate them or forget to include them in the application entirely. I once had a student who, at the age of 16, started a small retail site that cleared over $80k - he didn't even think to mention it until a week before we were ready to submit his application because "if it's less than $100k it wasn't really a successful business". Needless to say, we had to rewrite half his application to include this accomplishment, and it was one of the key achievements that helped him get in.

3. You have to be able to Summarize it in Two Sentences:
Most applications are all over the place. A President of the
Debate Team, who wants to go into Pre-Med, but volunteers
at a homeless shelter. This is not a clear narrative for an AO
to pick up on. Instead focus your application on some
carefully selected elements that follow the same theme. For
example, a nationally ranked tennis player, who teaches
tennis to underprivileged kids and who did a Materials
Science research project on the best materials to use in a
Tennis ball. Get it? That student certainly had dozens of other
accomplishments that don't fit that theme. Doesn't matter. He
emphasized the ones that do. When your AO can sum you up
in two sentences, you're easy to explain to the committee. If
you're easy to explain, you're easy to defend, and you're way
more likely to get in.

Application Framing Checklist:
- Can you sum it up in 2 sentences or less?
- Does your essay humanize you?
- Are your accomplishments featured?
- Do your Passion Project, Essays, and ECs all follow a "theme"?

CHAPTER 5

HOW TO WRITE A STELLAR COLLEGE ESSAY

CHAPTER 5 - How to Write a Stellar College Essay

What You'll Learn:
- Why you should hire a Pro to help with your Essay and Application
- What is the REAL prompt (no matter what you choose).
- How the "Why Us?" essay is really a "Why You?" essay.

Almost everything you were taught in High school about "How to Write" is wrong. As a result, the best way to write a College Essay is not by yourself. If you can afford it, you should hire a professional to help you because you can rest assured that your competition will. However, if you're going to try to write it yourself, make sure you do the following things:

1.Remember your Goal: The goal of a College Essay is to get the Reader to fall in love with you so they'll advocate on your behalf. When you waste an essay restating your resume, you've missed the point. Your job is to appeal to their emotions as powerfully as you can because people make decisions with EMOTION first and then use "logic" and "facts" to justify whatever they wanted to do anyway.

2.Know the Real Prompt: Regardless of which prompt you choose to answer, the REAL prompt is always "Why should I admit you?". If your essay doesn't present a clear, simple answer to that question, supported by the remainder of your application, you missed the mark. Think of it as a sales pitch where you're "selling" yourself to the university, not open mic night at the College Café.

3.Grab their Attention, Early: Don't wait until the 2nd paragraph to say something interesting. Your reader is spending 1-2 minutes at most reading your essay. They're already tired after having read a stack of 100's just like it. If you don't shock them awake, your essay will blend in with the bland, boring pile of steaming garbage they just read. If your 1st sentence doesn't cause shock and awe, you're doing it wrong.

CHAPTER 5 - How to Write a Stellar College Essay

4. Tell them a Hero Story, not a Trauma Story: You may think your trauma is special, but it's probably cliche. Ivy League readers have seen it all. Death, abuse, destruction, it doesn't matter. No matter how many times we tell them not to, SOMEONE is still going to write their essay about the "sportsball" injury they had to push through, as if no one has done that before. The problem with "Trauma" stories is that they present you as a "victim" of your circumstances, and no one rewards you for that. **Instead, use the trauma as a starting point to grab their attention, describe it for no more than a paragraph, and spend the rest of your essay talking about how you overcame it. That makes it a Hero Story.** When you show a college that you learned and grew in the face of a difficult experience, it shows that you have what it takes to succeed in college and beyond.

5. Avoid Metaphors: Some VERY prominent College Essay "Experts" advise students to write flowery essays with philosophical observations or extended metaphors. Even if you work with a pro, this almost always results in poorly executed "artsy" essays that tell the reader nothing meaningful about the candidate. Unless you're phenomenally talented (think "Letter S" girl or similar) you should tell a straightforward and personal story that shows the reader your best qualities.

6. Be Concise: If you only need 400 words to tell a compelling story, leave it at that. There is no requirement to fill up the 650 word limit just because they gave it to you. 99% of the time when a student brings me a draft, we can cut the word count by half and not lose any meaning. You will write a more interesting, powerful and effective essay by making it as short as you possibly can.

Pro Tip: Treat every word you eliminate like it's $100 in your pocket, because if you do the math that's actually what it's worth.

7. Use Simple Language: Simple language is persuasive. Every time you use a word beyond a 3rd grade level, you're making it harder for your reader to understand what you're saying. If they don't understand you, they can't relate to you and they won't fall in love with you. Keep it simple.

8. Tell them your "Why": If your reader walks away from the essay knowing "why" you work as hard as you do, and "why" you pursue your goals, you nailed it. If they understand your personal narrative and motivations, it will be much easier for them to justify your admission to their colleagues.

If you want to see some examples of amazing College Essays, the Harvard Crimson publishes a collection of their favorite accepted essays each year. For some of the best advice on effective writing, google "The Day You Became a Better Writer" by Scott Adams and read his blog.

Advice for Supplements:
1. Turn "Why Us?" into "Why You?": An Ivy knows that half the reason you want to go there is the name. When they ask "why us," they aren't asking you to prove your ability to google obscure Ivy League trivia on the university website. They want you to 1) identify features of the university that align with your experience and 2) show how that experience would make you a good fit. Reframing the question from "why us?" to "why you?" makes this a LOT clearer. For example, maybe you did Physics research in high school, and there's a Yale professor doing research in the same exact area. Maybe you visited and felt that the aspirations of students at Penn aligned with yours. Take your pick but **make the focus about how YOU fit in, not a recitation of random facts.**

2. The Diversity Essay: Avoid politics if at all possible. Focus your essay on a time when you tried something new, or experienced a new culture. Perhaps a time when you disagreed with a teammate about the solution to a problem and how you were able to find consensus. They want you to show intellectual curiosity and flexibility in this essay, so make that the theme.

3. The Additional Information Section: Most Ivies let you submit a resume separately, so don't waste the additional information section on that. Instead use it to discuss any adverse experiences that may have affected your grades in school **OR** write a second essay about an emotionally powerful topic. They gave you 650 words, so you should use that to the fullest.

College Essay Checklist:
- Did you tell them why they should accept you?
- Does your Essay humanize you?
- Did you tell them a Hero story?
- Is your Essay as short as possible?
- Did you use Simple language (5th grade max)?
- Did you tell them your "Why"?

CHAPTER 6

HOW TO STAND OUT IN IVY LEAGUE ADMISSIONS

CHAPTER 6 - How to Stand Out in Ivy League Admissions

What You'll Learn:
- What factors get you INTO an Ivy, and which ones keep you OUT.
- How a Passion Project will help you stand out.
- Why Ivies aren't impressed by a 4.0 GPA.

How do you stand out? Figure out what the herd is doing, then do the opposite.

The vast majority of Ivy League applicants are smart, hard working students who did exactly what their teachers asked of them. They think they're going to stand out by having a 4.1 GPA instead of a 4.0. If that's you it's going to be VERY hard to get in. Ivies want you to go beyond what was asked of you. **They want you to be different.**

Standing out in Ivy League admissions starts by **focusing on the parts of the application that will get you in**, while meeting the standard on the parts of your application that could keep you out.

Factors that can GET YOU INTO an Ivy:
- Passion Project
- Essay
- Awards
- Extracurricular Activities
- Letters of Recommendation

Factors that can KEEP YOU OUT of an Ivy:
- SAT/ACT Score
- GPA
- Rank
- Class Rigor

CHAPTER 6 - How to Stand Out in Ivy League Admissions

It's possible to write an essay that is so amazing, it gets you in by itself. The same is true for all the items on the first list. When trying to boost the strength of your application **you should be focusing primarily on the factors that "get you in" because there is no ceiling.** No matter how long you work on them, you can always make them better, and it will have a HUGE impact on your admissions odds.

The second list is just housekeeping. You should get a 1500+ SAT to apply to an Ivy, but going from a 1530 to a 1560 will not impress them at all. Every item on the second list has **a minimum threshold you need to pass,** but pushing beyond that will not help you at all. Getting your GPA to 3.8+ unweighted, being in the top 5% of your class and taking the hardest classes your school offers isn't impressive to an Ivy. **It's the bare minimum.**

Standardized Test Scores: Test scores are an important signal to a college that a student is academically capable. Applying with a 1500+ SAT score won't get you in by itself, but it will certainly put to bed any uncertainty about your academic record. Likewise, applying without a Test Score won't get you rejected but it will force the Admissions Office to place A LOT more weight on your class grades and extracurriculars. I always recommend that students try to get the highest score possible on the SAT/ACT so they have more of a cushion for that one "B" on their transcript or the competition that didn't go their way.

Competing against your classmates is a losing strategy. There are only 24 hours in a day and 100 points on a test. You're not going to get ahead by playing the same game everyone else is. Instead, **sidestep the competition through creativity.** Use a Passion Project to create a lane of your own where you have no competition.

CHAPTER 6 - How to Stand Out in Ivy League Admissions

A Passion Project is a long term independent project in an area you're talented in that you take on during high school, under the supervision of an expert mentor to accomplish a few main goals:

1. Show Ivies that you have an **aptitude** for a particular skill/subject.
2. Gain **recognition and awards** for your aptitude.
3. Gain stories and experience that will provide **something interesting to write about in your application.**

A Passion Project can be almost anything provided that it aligns with your long term goals and skills. If you want to study Business in college, start a Business or get an Internship. If you want to study Science, get involved in Science Research at a local university. If you want to go into Politics, volunteer for a campaign. **Take whatever dreams you had for life after college, and make them a reality today.**

One of my favorite projects that you can do for any field of interest is writing a book. 10 years ago, if you wanted to write a book, you needed a publishing deal, an agent, and a lot of money upfront. Today all you need is a laptop, an idea and the perseverance to get the job done. The advent of Self-Publishing through services like Amazon's Kindle Direct Publishing and On-Demand Printing have changed the game entirely. You can write a book, in high school, on ANY topic and get it published and printed in a week. Moreover, since **99% of people don't have the conscientiousness to complete a book,** the fact that it exists at all will be enough to "WOW" Ivy League Admissions.

Pro Tip: If you're Pre-Med or Pre-Law there are course requirements but no Major (study area) requirements. Consider majoring in something other than Bio/Chem if Pre-Med or something other than Politics, History or Econ if Pre-Law. It'll definitely help you stand out both for college and graduate school admissions.

31

Finding a Mentor: To find a Mentor for your Passion Project, you need to **Cold Email.** Make a list of any local university professor in an area you want to research and send ALL of them an email. The same applies to business owners for internships, doctors for shadowing, engineers for projects etc. **Expect to send out AT LEAST 100 emails before anyone responds.**

Putting It All Together

To get into an Ivy you must make your Reader fall in love with your application so they advocate on your behalf in committee. To do that you have to stand out, and that takes a lot of work. **You'll need amazing test scores and top grades so you don't get weeded out; and, on top of that, you need to complete a Passion Project, secure letters of recommendation, become a leader in clubs, win national competitions, and write a stellar essay.**

Feels like a lot to do in 4 years, doesn't it?

I wrote the Ivy League Roadmap to show you the best way to do it. It's a path to the Ivies without stress and fear. Where you can develop your talents to the fullest extent so that no matter what happens, you're all the better for having done the work. The next few chapters will lay out a clear plan of action for every year of high school, so you know exactly what to do, when to do it and why it benefits you. **The closer you follow the path, the closer you get to the Ivy League.**

The Roadmap starts here. Are you ready?

CHAPTER 7

TIMELINE FOR ADMISSIONS

CHAPTER 7 - Timeline for Admissions

What You'll Learn:
- The Ideal Timeline for Ivy League Admissions
- Why starting in 6th grade is a HUGE Advantage
- What you need to work on if you're LATE to the game

Here's an Ideal timeline for Ivy League Admissions:
- **6th Grade:** Attempt to skip ahead to Algebra 1, explore other talents in clubs. Start focused practice for sports if intent is to be a recruited athlete.
- **7th Grade:** Take Geometry and any Honors Classes available to you, begin SAT Prep if interested in attending summer Programs like Johns Hopkins' CTY.
- **8th Grade:** Take the SAT early and attend enrichment programs, use free time to explore interests further.
- **9th Grade:** Start taking AP/IB Classes if available, ensure maximum rigor of courses. Try clubs at school to see what you like, preferably ones that compete.
- **Summer after 9th Grade:** Select and begin working on your Passion Project, find a mentor to supervise you for the next few years. Take classes at local Community College (CC) to get a head start on project related skills (anything with coding is usually a good return on investment).
- **10th Grade:** Begin SAT Prep in earnest, PSAT score this year will be a good benchmark for National Merit Scholarship. Classes should be mostly AP/IB by this point. Clubs narrowed down to 2-3 main ones where you're on track for State/National level recognition. AP Prep should be taken very seriously, 5's in 9-10th Grade are impressive. Take the SAT for the 1st time in Dec, 2nd time in March and if desired score is not achieved try again in August.
- **Summer after 10th Grade:** Passion Project in full swing, should spend all free time implementing the project or taking courses that will build project relevant skills. Take the SAT in August as a backup.

34

CHAPTER 7 - Timeline for Admissions

- **11th Grade:** Prep for PSAT and score in top 5% at least to be NMSQT Commended. SAT should be done already, but if you must, take it again in December. Clubs/Sports should be yielding multiple state/national level awards, the Passion Project should be making local headlines. Almost all classes should be AP/IB with top scores. Relationship with mentor should feel like a 3rd parent. College list should be set by this point.
- **Summer after 11th Grade:** College Essay writing should begin in June and be completely done by August (essay prompts are public and rarely change, no excuses). Reach out to Recommenders by July informally, and formally as soon as Common App/Naviance open. Passion Project should be making major waves, resulting in a paper, patent or publication.
- **12th Grade:** Classes should be all AP/IB or max rigor available ("senioritis" is for people who peak in High School). National Merit winners announced at the beginning of the year. Apps should be on autopilot and submitted as soon as possible, even for Regular Decision. Interview prep should be frequent with questions and scenarios fully rehearsed. Mid-year reports should be stellar.
- **Ivy Day (End of March): Collect your acceptances and celebrate!!!**
- **Apr 12th Grade:** Visit schools and negotiate with financial aid. If using Ivy acceptance for leverage, be in constant contact with financial aid offices to secure awards.
- **May 12th Grade:** Commit to a school and take the summer off!

Don't panic! This is an **IDEAL** timeline, so the vast majority of students who attempt (and succeed) at Ivy League Admissions will not follow this exactly. The ideal timeline shows **you what to work on.** Let's look at strategies for each point in the timeline.

CHAPTER 8

WHAT TO DO BEFORE 9TH GRADE

CHAPTER 8 - What to do Before 9th Grade

What You'll Learn:
- Why Talent Stacking is the Path to Success
- How programs like CTY can help you get into an Ivy
- Why attending a "feeder" high school can make it HARDER to get in

Your time before 9th Grade should be spent doing 3 things primarily:

1.Exploring your talents: Notice how I said "talents" and not "interests". Everyone is born with talents. Maybe you're a great writer, a capable singer or a powerful athlete. Any of these can be an Ivy League admissions asset if you discover them and begin to hone them early. Remember you will get nowhere by pursuing areas where you're "interested" with no results. You will become "passionate" about the areas where you're successful.

2.Growing your discipline: Show Ivy League Admissions Officers that you're capable of rigor and hard work. This may mean getting up an hour earlier every day to study, learning a language from scratch, or taking on high school level classes in your middle school.

3. Making Connections: Most Ivy League schools are looking for students who can stand out both academically and socially. Make sure you have a network of influencers in your hometown or even nationally. This will give you an edge over others who may have similar academic qualifications. These contacts need not be limited to Ivy League alumni, but can include successful people from a variety of backgrounds and professions.

CHAPTER 8 - What to do Before 9th Grade

Here's how you get a head start on the admissions process:

- **Skip ahead in Math:** Typical "Honors" math sequences in the United States will have you taking Algebra 1 in the 8th Grade. Most of the world starts Algebra 1 in 6th grade, and it would be a huge advantage if you did too. Many schools will not offer the option; so look into virtual schools or tutoring to learn the material and then request the opportunity to test out.

- **Apply to advanced summer programs like CTY:** Many top schools offer summer programs with challenging courses to students who demonstrate excellence at an early age. Usually, you'll have to take the SAT early and score above a certain level to be admitted. These types of programs look great on a college application because they're an early marker of exceptional ability that you can build on all the way through high school.

- **Join a Club or Travel Team for a Sport:** Recruited Athletes have a massive advantage in Ivy League Admissions; and, to be recruited you have to start early. Beyond that, building a strong record of competitive success in a sport or a club shows that you can succeed at something difficult and will keep you physically healthy.

Implement some effective "Life Strategies":

1. Get/Stay Healthy: The "Halo Effect" is real and powerful. Healthy, relaxed and physically attractive people have a huge advantage in every competitive area and Elite College Admissions is no exception. You should be careful to avoid processed foods in your diet, exercise regularly (ideally through a sport so it also helps your application), and sleep 9+ hours every night. You may think that "burning the midnight oil" and pounding energy drinks is how successful people get ahead, but you'd be wrong. Good time management and scheduling will let you spread the work out to a reasonable level and keep your anxiety in check.

2. Systems over Goals: Once you set a goal, use a system to build in rewards so you can enjoy the process as you're getting there.

2. Systems over Goals (cont'd) Instead of saying "I have to get a 5 on this AP Exam," block off time for studying and note taking every day, buy a review book and do weekly practice tests. Use a "checkbox" system to give yourself a little reward every time you do something that should bring you closer to the goal and don't focus so much on the bigger picture.

3. Talent Stacking: Professional Athletes have a terrible life strategy. Imagine trying to be an NBA player. Maybe you're born as LeBron James and it all works out, but for every one of him there are 10,000 others who devoted their whole life to success in basketball, failed, and were left with nothing. In any single competitive area, only the top 1% of people (or less) really make it, and the rest are mediocre at best. You can sidestep this trap through Talent Stacking. **99% of successful people are not 1:1,000,000 talents in one area, but instead are the top 10% in a few independent areas that they combine in a way that makes them completely unique.** This allows them to sidestep the Lebron's of the world and be the best in a field of their own. A student who is in the top 10% of a sport, top 10% academically and top 10% in building social connections will be able to find a skill at the intersection of those three (School Sports commentator for example) where there is no competition and he can really show off. This will give you a much better chance of success in life, not just college admissions.

4. Use Affirmations: Affirmations are how you program reality so it gives you what you want. If you write the phrase "I, <Your Name>, will get into an Ivy League school" 5 times on a piece of paper every morning, it will refocus your brain so you notice opportunities that bring you closer to that state of being. Even if you think this is woo-woo nonsense, it costs you nothing to give it a shot and see for yourself.

For further reading on life and success strategy, I highly recommend the book **How to Fail at Almost Everything and Still Win Big** by Scott Adams.

CHAPTER 8 - What to do Before 9th Grade

Choosing a High School: The choice of where you attend high school determines the pool of students that admissions officers will compare you to when you apply. You might think that your odds are better at an elite private feeder school, but those students tend to be competitive so you'll have to work A LOT harder to stand out. At the same time, smaller public schools tend to have fewer opportunities to take advanced classes and compete at a national level, but because the standard is lower for them, you don't have to work as hard to be the best. After the first year or so, if you notice you're only an average student in your class despite your best efforts, consider changing schools.

Note: Changing high schools can deny you the opportunity to have a class rank in your new school. Keep this in mind when deciding to switch.

End of 8th Grade Checklist:
- Did you do well in the hardest classes your school offers?
- Have you finished at least Algebra 1?
- Do you know what areas you're talented in?
- Have you participated in enrichment programs like CTY?
- Did you practice Healthy habits and Success strategies?

CHAPTER 9

WHAT TO DO IN 9TH GRADE

CHAPTER 9 - What to do in 9th Grade

What You'll Learn:
- Why you should take the HARDEST classes possible.
- Why Social Media can get you REJECTED
- How skipping a year in Math can DOUBLE your odds of getting in

Beginning of 9th Grade Checklist:
- Are you at least taking Geometry with Algebra 1 completed?
- Have you taken a practice SAT?
- Do you know which areas (2-3 max) you're talented in?

If you're missing one of those, take care of it first, then come back and start on the rest.

If you're starting 9th Grade and you want to end up in the Ivy League here's what you should do:

1.DO NOT post on personal social media: This is basic risk management. Students we've coached have gotten rejected from Ivies because of some random post on social media that they thought was "fine" at the time. There are ZERO people who are proud of the things they said in public at the age of 14. Moreover, the line of what is "socially acceptable" discourse is changing every day. Things you think are "safe" to post today can get you rejected or fired a few years down the line. Even worse, that bikini pic you dropped to brag to your friends about your latest vacation can put you on the radar of Child Predators and worse. Not worth it. The safest route would be to delete the accounts entirely, but since almost no one will do that – AT LEAST don't post anything and wipe clean any accounts with posts. Anyone who cares about you can find out about your life directly.

CHAPTER 9 - What to do in 9th Grade

2. Max Rigor: Take the most rigorous classes offered by your school, no matter what topic that includes. AP/IB/Dual Enrollment, it doesn't matter. Just add them all until you're on pace with the top students in your class. Your grades should be on autopilot, and maintained at a 3.8+ GPA unweighted (think A- or higher or a 93+/100).

3. Skip a year ahead in Math: This will accomplish 3 main things: 1) You will have a huge advantage on the SAT/ACT because you will reach Algebra 2 faster and will have more time to prepare for either exam regardless of how you choose to do it. 2) It allows you to be exposed to more complex math concepts early so questions on exams like the SAT/ACT will seem easier, and classes like Physics will actually make sense. 3) It will give you a major advantage in math competitions and will make Community Colleges more open to letting you take courses as a non-matriculated student. The typical math progression for Ivy bound students is 8th: Algebra 1, 9th: Geometry, 10th: Algebra 2/ Trig, 11th: Pre-Calc and 12th: Calculus 1&2. If this looks like your current track, it can be a huge advantage to skip even 1 year ahead.

4. Try a LOT of Clubs but narrow down to 2-3 with High Commitment: It's impossible to predict which clubs you'll excel in unless you try them so in the beginning of the year attend as many as you can fit into your schedule. However, colleges do not reward you for "showing-up" to a dozen clubs. They want to see leadership, commitment and above all demonstrable accomplishments. This will be impossible to do if you spread yourself thin, so pick only 2-3 clubs (ideally 2 competition based, 1 service based) and go all in on those. Your impact in those clubs is what will impress a university down the line.

5. Begin SAT/ACT Prep: A 1500+ on the SAT or 34+ on the ACT does not happen overnight. You can drastically improve your odds of scoring that high if you start early. If you can afford it, the best way to learn the material is from a tutor or class. If you're going to self-teach through books or Khan Academy, it is even more important that you allow yourself extra time to prepare.

6. Meet with an Ivy League Admissions Advisor: Find a private advisor you trust and hire them for 1-2 hours to sit down with you and map out the next few years. Knowing exactly what to do for your specific case can save you thousands of dollars and hundreds of wasted hours.

7. Explore potential career paths: You should begin exploring potential career paths by visiting companies you'd like to work for, attending events related to your interests, or talking with mentors in areas you would like to pursue. **Caution: Passion is overrated.** If you're interested in something but have demonstrated no talent for it, you can keep it as a hobby but under no circumstances should it be the focus of the next few years. As an example, you may love to sing in the shower, but anyone who hears you begs you to stop. That's a great indicator that your efforts are better spent elsewhere.
Note: If you can **convince a stranger to PAY you for a service you provide**, that's a GREAT indicator that you're actually talented and you should pursue it further.

8. Choose a Passion Project and find a Mentor: By the end of 9th grade you should have a topic for the project picked out and should start learning the key skills you'll need to bring it to fruition. For example, if you want to study Computer Science, and your project is building an app, this is a great time to take an introductory coding class at a local community college.

CHAPTER 9 - What to do in 9th Grade

On Mentors: You should choose a mentor that is an expert on the thing you want to accomplish. Keep in mind that you should not expect the mentor to spoon-feed you knowledge, but rather provide guidance and resources for you to learn from. Maintaining the relationship with the mentor is as important as the success of the project as they will be writing your letter of recommendation when it's done.

Note for the Summer: The summer after 9th grade is best spent doing one of 3 things: 1) Attending pre-college enrichment programs like CTY 2) Taking classes to build skills you'll need for a passion project or competition 3) Executing on the plan for your Passion Project.

Definitely schedule in some time for fun and relaxation (you're still a kid after all), but 2-3 months of doing **SOMETHING** while your "competition" is doing **NOTHING** is a massive edge.

End of 9th Grade Checklist:
- Did you do well in the hardest classes your school allows?
- Have you begun SAT/ACT Prep?
- Did you meet with an Independent Counselor and chart a plan for the next few years?
- Have you chosen the 2-3 Clubs you'll be focusing on?
- Do you have an idea and a mentor for your Passion Project?

CHAPTER 10

WHAT TO DO IN 10TH GRADE

CHAPTER 10 - What to do in 10th Grade

What You'll Learn:

- Why volunteer HOURS don't matter, but IMPACT does.
- Why you should take the SAT early.
- Why 100's of volunteer hours WON'T help you get into an Ivy

Beginning of 10th Grade Checklist:

- Are you in the hardest classes your school allows?
- Have you started SAT Prep?
- Have you chosen and started your Passion Project?

If you're missing one of those, take care of it first, then come back and start on the rest.

If you're starting 10th Grade and you want to end up in the Ivy League here's what you should do:

1. Aim to take the SAT/ACT for the 1st time by December: Why so early? Test prep is a marathon, not a sprint. The best students expect to take the SAT/ACT at least 3-4 times before they're satisfied that their score has reached a plateau. Most students begin this process in 11th grade when they're already drowning in AP and IB classes and deprive themselves of the opportunity to study for it seriously. Some students will still be taking the SAT all the way up to the fall of their Senior year and give themselves a nervous breakdown as they write College Apps, study for AP/IB Classes AND do SAT Prep all at the same time. If you're my client, I won't allow you to make that mistake, so you take the SAT early. Aim to take the SAT for the 1st time in December, 2nd time in March and if your desired score is not achieved try again in August before 11th Grade.

2. Prepare for the PSAT/NMSQT: The version of the PSAT given in 10 & 11th grade is the same exam, and NO it is not a "Practice SAT" as many assume from the acronym.

2. Prepare for the PSAT/NMSQT (cont'd): The PSAT is a watered down version of the SAT scored much more heavily on the Verbal sections (Reading + Writing) than the Math which is used in 11th Grade to select the winners of the National Merit Scholarship competition. Winning the National Merit Scholarship can be worth $20k or more and is a major mark in your favor for Ivy League admission, so you should DEFINITELY try hard on the PSAT. Fortunately, the exam is similar to (and easier than) the SAT so doing SAT Prep early covers you for the PSAT too.

3. Max out on AP/IB/Dual Enrollment Classes: Colleges look at your course and standardized test grades VERY seriously from 10th Grade on. Getting a 5 on an AP Class in 10th Grade is very impressive because it's still early and doing poorly looks bad because it's not early enough. Do not take AP/IB exams lightly. Your score on those exams matters AT LEAST as much to an Ivy League School as your grade in the course and they will assume it's low if you don't report it.

4. Win State/National Awards in your Clubs/Competitions: By this point you should have some experience participating in Clubs/Competitions and particularly for organizations like AMC, DECA, Debate, FBLA, HOSA, 4H, Science Olympiad, ISEF etc. that have regional, state and national levels you should be racking up awards. The same goes for sports, though for team based ones this can be a bit harder depending on the quality of your teammates.

5. Volunteer Work: Impact matters more than hours spent for Volunteering. For example, one student might devote 100 hours to mentor students in an underprivileged school in robotics while another spends 20 hours making a dozen tutorial videos that get uploaded to YouTube and help 1000's of students around the world. Which student has the more compelling case? Obviously the 2nd one because he made a bigger IMPACT while doing something creative. Needless to say, this also frees up time to study for classes, competitions, and HAVE FUN. Don't waste your life volunteering for contrived events. Do a few things that matter and you'll get ahead.

6. Passion Project: 10th Grade is when your Passion Project should really start to take form. Schedule some time (2-3 hrs /week) to work on it so it doesn't impact your schoolwork and check in with your mentor at least once a month. At this point, if you're interested in a profession like medicine or law, you should look into Shadowing / Internship opportunities on the weekend or during the summer.

7.College Visits: Once you get an SAT/ACT score that confirms you have a serious shot at elite universities (1500+SAT/34+ ACT),start making the rounds to visit some of the schools you're interested in. A college visit is an opportunity to learn about the university up close and personal. Make sure to take note of particular details about the school that are unusual or obscure to leverage in your college essays down the line.

NOTE: Make sure you visit your "Safeties". **None of the Ivies take "demonstrated interest" through a college visit seriously** because they already know why you're interested. However, if you want to use an Ivy acceptance to leverage a scholarship from a lower ranked school, the lower ranked school likely WILL care that you visited. Lower ranked colleges often reject overqualified applicants to increase the percentage of admits who attend the school. Prevent being rejected by visiting; they will think you are serious.

Note for the Summer: The summer after 10th grade is best spent doing one of 3 things: 1) Working on your Passion Project 2) Taking classes to build skills you'll need for a Passion Project or competition 3) Visiting schools that interest you (both Ivies and targeted safeties).

End of 10th Grade Checklist:
- Did you do well in the hardest classes your school allows?
- Have you taken the SAT/ACT at least twice?
- Have you won any major awards or competitions?
- Have you made significant progress on your Passion Project?

WHAT TO DO IN 11TH GRADE

CHAPTER 11 - What to do in 11th Grade

What You'll Learn:
- Why you need to start your essays in June
- Why the PSAT can get you into an Ivy
- Why Rigor matters more than GPA

Beginning of 11th Grade Checklist:
- Are you in the hardest classes your school allows?
- Have you gotten a 1500+ on the SAT or a 34+ on the ACT?
- Is your Passion Project starting to yield results?

If you're missing one of those, take care of it first, then come back and start on the rest.

If you're starting 11th Grade and you want to end up in the Ivy League here's what you should do:

1. Score in the Top 1% of the PSAT/NMSQT: The PSAT given in 11th grade is the only one that counts for the National Merit Scholarship competition so prepare for it well and score in the top 1% so you can be at least a Semi-Finalist. This is easier than it sounds since the vast majority who take it are completely unaware of how important this exam is, both to your finances and your odds in elite college admissions. If you prepare well you have a pretty good chance of winning the whole thing. You'll also have to get a high score on the SAT/ACT to confirm your PSAT score but if you're following this plan that should already be taken care of.

2. Max out Rigor and GPA (but choose Rigor > GPA): Your 11th grade GPA and rigor will be used above all other years to judge if you can handle the curriculum at an Ivy League school, so take the hardest classes available and try to get a 4.0 unweighted (UW). You can often explain away a bad grade in 9th or 10th grade as "immaturity" but in 11th, unless you have a medical excuse and a perfect GPA the rest of the years, they WILL hold a GPA under a 3.8 UW against you.

2. Max out Rigor and GPA (but choose Rigor > GPA) (cont'd): Same goes with not taking the most rigorous course load your school offers. As long as it won't push your overall GPA below a 3.8, always choose the harder class over the 4.0 GPA. All A's in easy-medium classes are not as impressive as an A-/B+ in AP or IB.

Note: Ivies DO NOT CARE about one "C" on your transcript, as long as the rest are A's. Also, if your grades steadily improve from 9th grade on, it's as good as if they were high all along.

3. Push yourself in State/National Competitions: This is your time to shine. Devote as much effort and time as you can winning State and National competitions in the areas you've been pursuing for the past 2 years. By this point you should be a seasoned member of your team and should be spending time mentoring the underclassmen as you lead them to victory. This is your time to show colleges your leadership and teamwork abilities as you fight for a spot on their campus.

4. Get Elected to Leadership Positions: You should aim to end the year as the President or Captain of as many clubs as you can devote serious effort to. There's no sense in being a figurehead, so focus on clubs where your efforts will lead to tangible outcomes for your team. This won't be a huge factor that gets you IN to an elite school but if you don't have a few, they're going to wonder why.

Pro Tip: Avoid "Class President" roles or similar that devolve into a popularity contest unless you're sure you can win.

5. Harvest your Passion Project: By the end of the year your Passion Project should be complete or yielding some seriously impressive results. Your mentor should feel pretty close to you by this point, like having an extra parent. See if you can attract the interest of any local newspapers to write an article about your accomplishments and post widely on social media about your Project so you have a portfolio to present when it's time to apply. At this point your Letter of Recommendation should be in the bag.

6. Wipe your Personal Social Media: Again, pure risk management. Ivies look at the social media of applicants and you can't control what they think about what they find. Much safer not to have any at all, but at least delete/make private any posts and don't post anything new until you set foot on campus.

7. College Visits: At this point you should know if you're a serious candidate so use that information to select which schools you're visiting.

Summer after 11th Grade:
This is where the heavy lifting comes in for College Apps. Here's a timeline so you know how to handle it:

- **Late May/Early June:** As soon as you're done with school it's **time to start drafting your College Essays.** If you can afford to hire a pro to write them with you, you should. They'll come out much better than if you go it alone. If that's not an option, at least use the general College Essay Guide in the appendix and you'll be ahead of 90% of your competition. **Aim to have them all completed by late August**. If you are my client I REFUSE to let you miss this deadline, because you'll have enough application related responsibilities in the Fall and I don't want you to get stressed over something you can take care of early. Make sure you have talented writers (Journalists, Lawyers, anyone who gets paid to write) look them over.
- **Note:** Lazy people will object to the Early Deadline because the Common App doesn't open until August. They think the prompt might change, making some of you work irrelevant. This is nonsense. The prompts barely ever change, and you can find the ones from last year with a simple Google search. Even if they do change the work it takes to adapt an essay to a slightly changed prompt is WAY less than writing one from scratch under pressure.

- **Mid-July:** By this point you should informally (via email) reach out to all your recommenders to ask them to start drafting you a letter of recommendation. They'll devote a lot more effort to it if you let them start in the summer and hold it in reserve instead of waiting until they're slammed with similar requests in the fall.
- **August:** By this point your essays should be done and as soon as the Common Application opens you should take care of all the demographics and upload as many essays and supplements as possible. Request your recommenders and transcripts formally through Common App or Naviance, whichever your school is using.
- **Throughout**: Keep working on the final phases of your Passion Project, Research Project or Internship. Maintain relationships with your mentors to ensure your recommendations are good.

Note on Letters of Recommendation: A letter of recommendation is a point of social proof for Admissions Officers. If a smart, influential person went out of their way to write a letter supporting you, it makes you a less risky candidate. Odds are, the person reading your application will never meet you, so **they rely on these letters to confirm the good character traits in your application** and to cover them if they stick their neck out on your behalf. This is why getting letters from famous and powerful people can be a huge boost to your application. The implied logic is that by admitting you, they're doing a small favor to that powerful person, who in turn could help the university later on.

End of 11th Grade Checklist:
- Did you do well in the hardest classes your school allows?
- Did you get a 1500+ on the SAT or a 34+ on the ACT?
- Did you score in the top 1% on the PSAT?
- Have you won any major awards or competitions?
- Have you completed your Passion Project?
- Are your essays drafted?
- Did you request your Letters of Recommendation?

CHAPTER 12

WHAT TO DO IN 12TH GRADE

CHAPTER 12 - What to do in 12th Grade

What You'll Learn:
- How to Prep for Interviews
- Why submitting ALL your applications early can BOOST your odds
- How you can leverage an Ivy acceptance for a FULL RIDE at another school

Beginning of 12th Grade Checklist:
- Are you in the hardest classes your school allows?
- Have you drafted your essays and supplements?
- Have you completed your Passion Project?
- Do you have a 1500+ SAT score or 34+ ACT Score?

If you're missing one of those, take care of it first, then come back and start on the rest.

If you're starting 12th Grade and you want to end up in the Ivy League here's what you should do:

1. **Get your Applications in Early:** The Common App allows for submissions as early as August going into 12th Grade. Your applications for both Early Action, Early Decision and Regular Decision should all go in as close to that deadline as possible. Why? An admissions officer spends an average of 3-5 minutes reading most essays and applications. **Wouldn't you rather they had hours to blow with nothing better to do than give you the full consideration your hard work deserves?** That's what happens when you apply in August/September, a full month ahead of most applicants. Also, provided your application gets sorted into the top tier, you can rest assured that lack of open spots won't get you rejected. This early, every spot is open.

Note: If you're starting late, you're always better off submitting a polished application closer to the deadline than submitting a rushed application early. Take your time and do it right.

2. Prep for Interviews: If you see a politician or actor appear totally cool as they answer questions about their background, that's not an accident. There is a 100% chance that they've had professional media training and have rehearsed every possible question they could be asked a dozen times over. You may think this type of rehearsal would make you come off dry or robotic but the opposite is true. **If you're well prepared and relaxed in your interviews it gives you the freedom to be creative and funny on the spot.** This is important, as your Alumni Interviews are a chance to get a stellar letter of recommendation from someone the Admissions Office trusts. If you do it well it could be the final push you need to land firmly on the Admit List. Always follow each interview with a personalized thank you note.

3. Keep Up the Max Rigor and GPA: Senioritis is for people who peak in High School. If that were you, you wouldn't be reading this. If you want a good shot at Ivy League Admissions your Mid- Year Report (sent in January) needs to reflect the same High Rigor and GPA that you've maintained for the past few years. You can let off the gas (a little) once this report goes out, but keep in mind that any significant drop in your grades can lead to your Acceptance being rescinded even if you do get in.

4. Stay in Contact with your Regional AO: Every elite university has 2-3 Admissions Officers assigned to each region of the country and responsible for reading the applications from that region. There are always crazy Type A students that will email their regional AO non-stop and tank their admissions odds, so don't be one of them. Instead, limit your communications to major updates and accomplishments that might move the needle on your application.

4. Stay in Contact with Regional AO (cont'd): For example, if you did Science Research and your paper was accepted for publication after you submitted your application, you should definitely let them know. If you got an "A" on your Calc test last week you can safely keep that to yourself.

Then you wait, check the portal and: **YOU GOT IN!!! WOOOOOOO!!!!! Congratulations!**

Once you get in shift your focus to the following:
1. Maintain GPA: Keep your GPA at least above a 3.5 in all classes so you don't set off any alarm bells that would get your application rescinded.

2. Visit the Schools you're Admitted to: If you're admitted to a large number of schools, a visit can be a great way to narrow down the list; and, admitted student days tend to be a very fun experience even if you choose not to go so don't miss them.

3. Negotiate Financial Aid: Every year there are plenty of students who get into Ivy League schools but can't go because the Financial Aid provided won't cover their expenses. If that's you, try to negotiate with the office and see if there are any other scholarships you can apply for through the school. If you got in through ED there isn't a whole lot you can do to change it (which is why ED students generally get less financial aid), but if you have multiple RD Acceptances to Top 20 schools, you can probably get them to budge a little.

4. Send LOCI: If you were placed on a Waitlist for a school you wanted to attend, send them a Letter of Continued Interest (LOCI) describing any accomplishments you've racked up since applying and expressing your desire to attend. This is unlikely to move the needle unless you win major awards in the interim, but it's worth trying regardless.

CHAPTER 12 - What to do in 12th Grade

5. Use your Ivy Admit as Leverage at a Lower Ranked School: Especially if you got into multiple Ivies through RD, you can use the offers to leverage a better scholarship at a lower ranked school. Often schools that are still ranked in the Top 50 Nationally will throw Full Tuition scholarships at you just to snatch you from the Ivies. To achieve this, go to their Financial Aid office (ideally in person) and offer to commit to the lower ranked school on the spot if they give you a significantly better scholarship. Some schools will refuse to negotiate, but most will boost your offer on the spot.

That's the end of the Ivy League Roadmap. You can chart your own course from here and use the foundational skills you built through this process to help you do it. Good luck!

CHAPTER 13

HOW TO WORK WITH ANDREAS

CHAPTER 13 - How to work with Andreas

Andreas and the team behind the Ivy League Roadmap **only work with about 50 Families per year**. This number is capped to ensure that we can devote our full attention to those clients. We're selective with our clients as we want to devote our efforts only to families who will take full advantage of the expertise and opportunities we provide. **We only work with Clients who are fully committed to our process and who understand the value of our service as an investment in their future.**

If you're interested in working with Andreas you can scan the following QR Code and fill out an application. If we think you're a good fit we will reach out to offer you a spot in our program. Good luck!

SCAN ME
or visit www.ivyroadmap.org

CHAPTER 14

TRANSFER ADMISSIONS

CHAPTER 14 - Transfer Admissions

What You'll Learn:
- What you can do to stand out.
- Why you NEED a 4.0 GPA.
- Why you should build relationships with professors.

If you're starting as a Transfer Student and you want to end up in the Ivy League here's what you should do:

1. Accept the Odds: Transferring into an Ivy League School is at least 10x harder than getting in out of High School. Ivies have a strong preference for students doing the full 4 years there and will only admit a student on Transfer if there's a strong reason to do it.

2. Finish Strong in High School: The most common profile of a student admitted through transfer is a student who almost made it in the freshman admissions process but needed to fix a few small parts of their application. So, if you don't get in the 1st time around, make sure you don't let off the gas your senior year of high school, giving them a strong academic record to consider.

3. Go to the Highest Ranked School you got into: The easiest way to transfer into an Ivy is from another Ivy. The second easiest way is from a school ranked just below them. If you were admitted to a number of colleges, but rejected from your top choice; and you want to transfer in, you'll have a much easier time transferring from a prestigious school where high grades will be taken seriously.

4. Get a 4.0 GPA in College: Your college GPA will be weighted even more heavily than your high school GPA in Transfer Admissions. Use this to your advantage and make up for any shortcomings in High School by getting a 4.0. You're an adult now, so no excuses.

5.Make sure your Credits will Transfer: Check if the university you're attending has an Articulation Agreement with the university you want to transfer into. If not, you may end up having to retake a lot of classes you already completed.

6. Build Relationships with your Professors:

Recommendations for transfers come from your Professors the way that recommendations in high school come from your Teachers. The difference in college is that your Professors can also be your research mentors and supervisors. You can use that involvement to build a strong relationship with them and enhance your letters of recommendation.

7. Prepare your Reason: If you're already at a good university, you'll need to come up with a better reason for transferring than "more resources at an Ivy". Location, a particular professor, or other personal connection to the university can provide that. Be ready to justify why you'd be a good fit there.

8. Consider Hiring a Professional: Transfer Admissions is VERY hard. If you can afford it, do not try to go it alone. Your essays need to be persuasive, and that's extremely hard to do as a college student with limited experience writing at that level. A professional can also tell you what you did wrong in your original applications so you can shore up those weaknesses this time around.

Transferring into an Ivy League school is a challenge, but success is possible with the right approach. Consult a professional to see if transferring is a good choice for you.

Transfer Student Checklist:
- Did you score a 1500+ on the SAT or 34+ on the ACT?
- Do you have a 4.0 GPA?
- Do you know which professors will recommend you?
- What's your reason for Transferring?

CHAPTER 15

INTERNATIONAL ADMISSIONS

CHAPTER 15 - International Admissions

What You'll Learn:
- Why your High School grades WON'T be trusted
- Why you NEED a Passion Project
- Why you can boost your odds by NOT applying for Financial Aid

Your odds when applying to an Ivy League school as an International student depends a lot on your citizenship status. If you're a U.S. citizen who just happened to attend high school abroad, you will be considered the same as a domestic applicant and might even have a leg up if your high school is less well known. If you're not a U.S. citizen the following things change:

1. You'll be subject to Country/Continent Quotas: Ivy League schools only allocated a limited number of spots each year for non-U.S. citizen students. This is usually no more than 10% of the incoming class despite making up a significant chunk of applicants. The competition for these spots is fierce and significantly harder if you're from a competitive continent like Asia, but much easier from an underrepresented continent like Africa.

2. You will be ineligible for most Financial Aid: Since most Financial Aid (even at Ivies) is directly or indirectly subsidized by the U.S. Government, they are bound to disburse it only to U.S. citizens. There are some institutional grants that are specifically for international students but they're only given to a handful of students each year. Definitely check on the schools you're interested in to see what aid you'll be eligible for as it varies widely and changes often. **Note:** Especially as an international applicant, you can increase your odds of admission by not requesting financial aid.

3. You may not be able to legally stay in the U.S. after you graduate: You can stay in the U.S. if you 1) Get a job in the U.S. and your employer agrees to sponsor you or 2) You get married to a U.S. Citizen. Make sure you have a plan for where you will live and work before you graduate.

CHAPTER 15 - International Admissions

Most of my advice for international students is the same as for domestic applicants with the following exceptions that apply regardless of citizenship status:

1.They won't trust your grades from High School: U.S. Colleges including the Ivy League, are wary of rampant grade inflation and cheating on High School grades. They will value a high score on the SAT or ACT far more than high grades in high school, because it's harder to fake. You can achieve something similar by attending a school with an IB, or similar international curriculum that has objective standards for grading. **Note:** This may feel unfair if you go to a school that grades even HARDER than U.S. High Schools, so try to understand it from their perspective. There's no way for them to investigate every high school in the world so they know who to trust. The tests are the only way to handle the problem at scale.

2. You may not have access to Clubs, so focus on a Passion Project: Clubs in High School are a primarily American trait. If you attend a high school outside the U.S. you may not have clubs and especially not clubs that compete. If that's the case you should focus on your Passion Project to compensate. Start this project as early as possible so you have time to accomplish something significant before you apply.

3.You may need to take the TOEFL: If your country of origin doesn't speak English, many U.S. universities will require you to take and score high on the TOEFL exam to confirm that your command of English is good enough to attend classes here. The exam is a VERY low bar so if you have trouble with it, you may want to reconsider going to school in the U.S. because the classes are definitely harder. Look up the requirements for the schools you're interested in before you apply.

4. You'll have better odds if you DON'T apply for Financial Aid: Ivies make a TON of money off International Students (particularly non-U.S. citizens) who pay the full ticket price for Tuition and Housing. If your family has the means, you should indicate on your application that you won't be seeking financial aid.

5. Visit the U.S. before you Apply: Living in the U.S. is not for everyone. You'll be far from your friends and family, will likely eat different food than you're used to and may speak a language other than your native one. There is a very real possibility that you'd be happier at a university in your country of origin. So if you can, visit the U.S. a few times before you apply so you know if it's a good fit for you.

International Applicant Checklist:
- Did you score a 1500+ on the SAT or 34+ on the ACT?
- Have you taken the TOEFL?
- Did you do an amazing Passion Project?
- Can your family afford the Full Price?
- Have you visited the U.S.?

CHAPTER 16

FAQS

- **I got some bad grades because of a Medical Issue, where can I explain that?**
  - That's what the Additional Information section of the Common App is for! Write about it there, have your guidance counselor confirm it and make sure the rest of your grades are amazing.
- **What do I do if I get rejected?**
  - Go to the best school you can for the lowest cost you can. Your success in life is not determined by College Admissions. I've seen some spectacular students who did everything right STILL get rejected from ALL 8 Ivies. It happens sometimes, but it never once held them back in life because they built the skills they need to succeed.
- **Can I take easier classes and still get into the Ivy League?**
  - Sure. You can also run a marathon without preparation. It won't be easy and you'd be much better off if you prepared as intensely as you can.
- **Do you have any suggestions of topics for my Passion Project?**
  - Absolutely. I wrote a small book with ideas and advice on how to execute it which you can download from at: https://stan.store/ivy_roadmap
- **When should I start preparing for the SAT?**
  - As soon as you finish Algebra 2. There are competitive summer programs that require an SAT score as early as the summer after 7th grade. To be adequately prepared for these challenges, you need to start preparing in 6th Grade, but otherwise you can wait for Algebra 2.
- **What is the PSAT?**
  - It is a slightly easier version of the SAT administered in 10th and 11th grade. In 11th grade your results are used for the National Merit Scholarship—meaning—you can win thousands of dollars if you score within the top 1% on the PSAT.

CHAPTER 16 - FAQs

- **How do I decide if I should send my SAT/ACT score to a school?**
  - Look up the 25th Percentile SAT/ACT score for a school you're applying to. If your score is higher than that, send it.
- **What's a National Merit Scholar?**
  - A person who scores within the top 1% within their state on the PSAT.
- **What SAT score do I need to be a competitive applicant?**
  - 1500+. This puts you within the top 1% of applicants. The SAT is used as a benchmark. You must meet the requirement to even be considered.
- **Is Khan Academy a Good tool for the SAT?**
  - Yes, but only if you already have a 1400+ on the SAT. It is good for refining skills. For learning entirely new skills, you should just take a class or hire a tutor.
- **Which is better: SAT or ACT?**
  - They are the same in the minds of a college admissions officer. Just pick your favorite and score a 1500+ or a 34+ on the respective exam.
- **Which is better: AP or IB?**
  - They are the same in the minds of a college admissions officer. Just pick your favorite and do well in the class.
- **How many APs/IBs/College Classes should I take?**
  - You want to make your schedule as rigorous as possible in relation to your interests. The more the better as long as you are willing to work hard.
- **What AP Score do I need to get into an Ivy?**
  - Mostly 5s, 4's are okay. 3s and below would look poorly on your application.
- **Is being in an institution like Mensa something Colleges will like?**
  - Not really. They want to see that you have worked hard to attain your current position, not that you assume superiority over people due to your natural ability.

- **What if my SAT Score is really high (say 1560) but I have a low GPA (say 3.3), can I still get into the Ivy League?**
  - Yes. However, you must have very good reasons to explain your shortcomings in terms of gpa. Usually colleges will give you a space to explain some bad grades on your application, so you must take advantage of this.
- **What if I have all As but a low SAT Score (say 1300)?**
  - This will show colleges that your school may not be as rigorous as other schools, meaning that your grades mean less. It will hurt your chances at admission into the Ivy League.
- **When should I take Algebra I?**
  - 6th Grade.
- **When should I take Algebra II?**
  - 8th Grade.
- **When should I take Calculus?**
  - 9th Grade.
- **How many letters of Recommendation do I need?**
  - At least two. Preferably from teachers that have a personal connection to you, not just ones where you got an A in their class.
- **How do I make a good Resume?**
  - Google the template from Harvard and use that.
- **How many essays will I have to write for the Common App?**
  - Depends on the number of colleges you apply to. You have to write the common app essay and then 2-3 short essays for each application on average.
- **What should I write my Common App essay on?**
  - A unique experience/passion project that allows you to stand out to the admissions officer. Avoid commonly used topics or struggles. If the admissions officer is bored, they will not rate your application as high as they could have otherwise.

CHAPTER 16 - FAQs

- **How do I prepare for an interview?**
  - Write out answers to commonly asked interview questions.
  - Remember your goal is to make friends with the interviewer.
  - Practice answering questions on your feet.
    - DECA/Debate Team are great clubs to practice this skill.
- **Does being Test Optional hurt my chances at admission?**
  - No, if your extracurriculars and passion project are fantastic and you have a lot of awards. Otherwise, it looks like a hole in your application.
- **Can't anyone self-publish a book as a Passion Project? Wouldn't universities know that so it doesn't mean much?**
  - No, it means a lot. Just because anyone can do it doesn't mean they will. Most people won't and publishing a book will really help you stand out.
- **How should 9th graders map out a path to college?**
  - Read this book.
- **How do I get involved in research?**
  - Look for opportunities within your school/community first. There are also programs at local universities where they allow high school students the opportunity to do research. Look out for both of these, and if not make a list of every professor at your local university in departments that interest you and mass cold-email them. If you email 100, 1 will respond.
- **Does an Instrument help you get into the Ivy League?**
  - Yes, if you do something creative with it–i.e. Start a YouTube channel playing your violin. Unless you do something like this, you will just be another fish in a very large pond.
- **Can starting a Business help me get into an Ivy?**
  - Absolutely, and it's a useful life skill regardless. Make it successful and it can be the centerpiece of your Essay and Application.

ACKNOWLEDGEMENTS

I want to give a huge thank you to my girlfriend Sophia who helped design this book, to my brother Nicholas who helped me assemble it, to my friend and mentor Adam who always gives me confidence and clarity in my decisions, to my friend Vito for helping me find the velocity to complete this, and to my Parents for their constant support.

Made in the USA
Columbia, SC
02 January 2025

51060151R00046